10
STEPS TO
Happy!
THOUGHT PROCESSING JOURNAL

VERONICA CLANTON-HIGGINS, MSW

10 STEPS TO

Happy!

THOUGHT PROCESSING JOURNAL

10 Steps to Happy

Copyright © 2019 by Veronica Clayton-Higgins

Book Design by Allison Arnett of www.branditbeautifully.com

ISBN 978-1-975-61296-2

Dedication

This book is for the YOU. The one who often feels unheard, unseen, and lost in this world full of facades. This book is for YOU. The one who tries to smile through her hurt, who wants to be happy but does not know where to start. This book is for you Sis. Use this book to tap into yourself so you can start the journey of happiness and wellness. Happy exists within you.

Table of Contents

Disclaimer

The information provided in this book is designed to provide helpful information on the subjects discussed. This book is not meant to be used, nor should it be used, to diagnose or treat any mental health or medical condition. For diagnosis or treatment of any mental health or medical problem, consult with a licensed therapist or physician. The author is not responsible for any specific health needs that may require medical supervision and is not liable for any damages or negative consequences from any treatment, action, application or preparation, to any person reading or following the information in this book.

Greetings

Life can be complicated.

Juggling many tasks and responsibilities can leave one feeling overwhelmed. How does one find that happy place? That place between stress and not stressed. That place where you can exist in a perpetual state of peace. The purpose of this journal is to start you on the path to finding your happy. To discover the things that make you smile and bring you a sense of balance. Use this journal as a tool to build the foundation of your well-being. You can do the steps in the order that feels good to you. Change takes time. Refer back to this journal when you are feeling stressed or your mind is flooded with negative thoughts. Allow it to guide you to that sacred space that only you can create.

Your journey begins...now.

Be blessed beloved.

Veronica

How to Use this Journal

This thought processing journal was created to help you BEGIN the process of unlocking your inner peace, to find your place of Happy.

- There are 10 affirmations. Say these at least 3 times a day. Out loud. Let your brain hear what your heart is doing.

- There are 10 Journal activities. Read each one carefully before completing the exercise. Make sure that you are relaxed and ready to complete the activity.

- There is 1 mindfulness exercise. This teaches you to calm your brain when negative thoughts try to steal your happy. Practice this as often as you feel is needed.

- There is 1 Vision Board page. You can draw, write, doodle, or cut out images that represent what happiness looks like to you.

- You do not have to do the activities in order. Choose the order that works best for you.

Step One

"I release *all* *thoughts* that no longer serve me well."

Purge your negative thoughts.
Write down any negative thoughts that invade your mind, then....

CROSS THEM OUT! VOID those thoughts!

They have no place in your energetic space.

You control your thoughts. They don't control you.

Now go and be Fabulous.

Action: Purge Bad Thoughts

"Right now, I *choose* to be at *peace* with myself."

Sometimes negative thoughts occur when we feel overwhelmed or not in control. Meditation/prayer can help calm your thoughts.

Meditation= listening to your higher power
Prayer= your higher power is talking to you.

Take a moment to sit in silence. Clear your mind. Let the positive thoughts flow through. Write down what comes to your mind. Pay attention to how you feel emotionally, physically, and spiritually after you are done. When you are having a rough day refer back to this page.

Action: Silence

"I am what I think, so I *choose* to think *positive* thoughts."

What are some negative thoughts that invade your mental space?
Write them down... then re-write them as a positive.

FOR EXAMPLE
Negative: "Man, my life totally sucks!"
Positive: "My life isn't perfect, but I am grateful for_____"

Life is not always rainbows and unicorns, however our thoughts can have a huge impact on how we navigate our daily lives. Just like one trains for the Olympics, you have to train in positive thoughts!

Negative:_____

Positive:_____

Negative:_____

Positive:_____

Negative:_____

Positive:_____

Action: Re-Train

 Vision Board

Use this blank page as a canvas for your HAPPY.
Draw. Write. Doodle.
Express what Happiness looks like to you.

Step Four

"I use my *focused energy* to cancel out negative thoughts."

What is an activity that improves your mood?
Mood enhancing activities also work to cancel out negative
thoughts.
Singing? Dancing? Yoga?
If you have an activity, describe below how you transform when you
are doing it.
How do you feel?
When was the last time you did it?
How often would you like to do it?
If you don't have an activity, now is the time to create one!

Action: Focused Energy

Step Five

"*I let go* of all tension that is within me."

1. Sit comfortably in a quiet place.

2. Start by breathing in and out slowly, for about 5 seconds.

3. Breathe in through your nose and out through your mouth, letting your breath flow effortlessly in and out of your body.

4. Focus on the way your body feels in this moment. Let your thoughts rise and fall with the inhale/exhale of your breath.

5. Allow all the negative thoughts and energy to exit your being with each exhale.

6. On the inhale, focus on bringing in positive thoughts and energy.

7. Do this whenever you are feeling tense or when your negative thoughts invade your space.

In the space below, write or draw about how you feel AFTER you have done this exercise.

Action: Just Breathe

"Today, I *choose to be* mindful of the things that make me happy!"

Mindfulness is a great way to discover your happy.
Mindfulness basically means the act being aware of yourself, your feelings, your environment in the present moment.
It can also be used to control negative thoughts.
When you find yourself being attacked by a negative thought that is attempting to disrupt your happiness.
STOP! Take a moment.
Tell yourself: "This thought does NOT serve my greater good!"
Close your eyes and exhale.
Release the negativity.
Pay attention to how you feel in this moment.
As you go through your day today, take some time to be mindful of the moments that resonate with you.
Was there a special song playing that made you smile?
A particular scent that jogged a memory?
In the space provided below, write about the moment that stood out to you and why it made you happy.

Action: Be Mindful

Mindfulness Square

If mindfulness is difficult for you because you are easily
distracted...use this Mindfulness square.
Focus on the square as you take deep breaths.
Feel your chest rise and fall with each breath.
Enjoy the sensation of being alive and free.
Continue to focus on the square and slowly tune out the sounds
around you.
Pay attention to the color, size, length of the square.
Isn't this square awesome?
Now continue to look at it, focusing on all it's awesome qualities.
Close your eyes.
Continue to take slow relaxing breaths, as you see the square in
your mind.
Wow...you just did a mindfulness exercise.
You rock!

"My mind is *now free* as I release any worries of not being loved."

You can change that negative soundtrack in your head by learning to talk to yourself in a friendly, positive way.

Having trouble?

Imagine what your best friend or family member would say to perk you up.

Supportive self-talk can help improve your mood by reminding you about all the wonderful qualities that make you special.

You're AMAZING... who wouldn't love you!

In the space provided below, write down all the great things your loved one would say about you.

Even better: **CALL** your loved one and **ASK** them what they think is great about you. Return the favor by sharing what you love about them.

Write what they shared below. Refer back to this when you need a mood booster.

Action: Give love. Be loved.

Step Eight

"I leave negativity *behind me* and never look back."

Happiness is something that YOU create!
Sort of like a recipe for your favorite meal.

You know all the ingredients needed to make the dish POP!

Happiness is a recipe for your well-being.
The ingredients for your happiness recipe:
Mirror Mantra + Favorite Song

Create a mantra to recite in the mirror to inspire you when you feel
negative thoughts creeping in.
In the space provide below.
Write your mantra.
Choose your fav song.

Now...Remix your mantra to the vibe of your favorite song!
Get that good energy flowing!

MANTRA

_____

_____

FAV SONG

_____

_____

MANTRA REMIXED TO FAV SONG

_____

_____

Action: Create Your Happy!

Thought Checking

Ask yourself these **SIX** Questions when you feel a negative thought trying to disrupt your peace.

- Is there any evidence to support this thought?

- Is there any evidence that disputes what I am thinking?

- Do my thoughts match the situation?

- What can I do to look at this in a more positive, but realistic manner?

- Will this matter in a few hours? Days? Weeks?

- What would I say to a friend who was having these same exact thoughts?

Step Nine

"I allow my thoughts to drift to a *positive* and *peaceful* place."

Inner peace is all about Self Care.
It takes time to develop a true sense of Inner Peace.
By recognizing the things that disrupt your Inner Peace,
you remain in control of your happy by avoiding
certain situations and / or people.
Remember, those you invite into your space can affect your
Inner Peace, which in turn affects your happiness.
Remember, you cannot control what others do.
You can only control your response.
In the box below, brainstorm some people and/or situations
you need to avoid in order to maintain your Inner "G"

[Inner Guru or Gangsta. You decide. ☻]

Action: Find your Inner "G"

"I will awaken *each day* with an attitude of gratitude."

Gratitude!

Yasssss! Gratitude is amazing!

Being grateful can improve your perception of life.
How you perceive things is how you receive things.
Having gratitude for the small things helps build up your happy muscles.

An attitude of gratitude can also help to reduce stress!
Below, list 10 things that you are grateful for.

1. _____

2. _____

3. _____

4. _____

5. _____

6. _____

7. _____

8. _____

9. _____

10. _____

Action: Be Grateful!

CONGRATS!

You have completed the 10 STEPS TO *Happy!*

You rock!

About the Author

Veronica Clanton- Higgins, MSW, is an author, educator, life coach, motivational speaker, and CEO of VCH Prosperity Consulting. A native of Compton, CA, Veronica is known for her community advocacy, support & healing of women, and youth mentorship. Veronica started VCH Prosperity Consulting in 2016 to address the social, emotional, and spiritual needs of women in her community. This was accomplished through the use of workshops that focused on connecting women through sisterhood. Her unique style of Life Coaching is a combination of empowerment, motivation, and inspiration. She has made it her life's purpose to improve the lives of others by helping them discover their self-worth through the use of mindfulness and self-affirming techniques.

Love & Gratitude

Made in the USA
Las Vegas, NV
22 July 2023

75098340R00026